¡Mírame, ahí voy! / Watch Me Go!

MI MONOPATÍN
MY SKATEBOARD

Victor Blaine

Traducido por Eida de la Vega

PowerKiDS press.

New York

Published in 2015 by The Rosen Publishing Group, Inc.
29 East 21st Street, New York, NY 10010

First Edition

Editor: Sarah Machajewski
Book Design: Mickey Harmon
Spanish Translator: Eida de la Vega

Photo Credits: Cover, p. 1 Daniel Milchev/Getty Images; p. 5 Lucidio Studio, Inc./Getty Images; p. 6 fotografos/Shutterstock.com; p. 9 corey mckenna/Thinkstock.com; p. 10 Fred Sweet/Shutterstock.com; p. 13 pio3/Shutterstock.com; p. 14 (main) lzf/Shutterstock.com; p. 14 (inset) Ray Mickshaw/Contributor/WireImage/Getty Images; p. 17 Galina Barskaya/Shutterstock.com; p. 18 Sino Images/Getty Images; p. 21 Tomasz Trojanowski/Shutterstock.com; p. 22 FogStock/Thinkstock.com.

Library of Congress Cataloging-in-Publication Data

Blaine, Victor.
My skateboard = Mi monopatín / by Victor Blaine.
p. cm. — (Watch me go! = ¡Mírame, ahí voy!)
Parallel title: ¡Mírame, ahí voy!.
In English and Spanish.
Includes index.
ISBN 978-1-4994-0278-0 (library binding)
1. Skateboarding — Juvenile literature. I. Title.
GV859.8 B53 2015
796.22 —d23

Manufactured in the United States of America

CPSIA Compliance Information: Batch #CW15PK: For Further Information contact Rosen Publishing, New York, New York at 1-800-237-9932

CONTENIDO

CONTENTS

Montar un monopatín es muy divertido. ¡Los monopatines se mueven muy rápido!

Riding a skateboard is a lot of fun. Skateboards move very fast!

Todos los monopatines tienen dos partes. Una parte es la **plataforma** y la otra son las ruedas.

All skateboards have two parts. One part is the **deck**. The other part is the wheels.

Para montar en monopatín hay que pararse sobre la plataforma. Las ruedas están debajo de la plataforma.

Skateboard riders stand on the deck. The wheels are under the deck.

A los que montan en monopatín se les llama monopatinadores.

People who ride skateboards are called skateboarders.

A los monopatinadores les gusta hacer trucos. Hay un truco que se llama *ollie*.

Skateboarders love to do tricks. One trick is called an ollie.

Alan Gelfand

El truco *ollie* se le ocurrió a un hombre llamado Alan Gelfand. Fue el primero que lo hizo.

A man named Alan Gelfand came up with the ollie. He was the first one who did this trick.

Los monopatinadores practican
sus trucos en un parque
de monopatín.

Skateboarders practice their
tricks at the skate park.

El parque de monopatín más grande del mundo está en China.

The largest skate park is in China.

Montar monopatín es divertido, pero es fácil lastimarse. Usa **casco**, **coderas** y **rodilleras** para protegerte.

Skateboarding is fun, but it's easy to get hurt. Wearing a **helmet** and **pads** helps you stay safe.

¿Qué más sabes sobre los monopatines?

What else do you know about skateboards?

PALABRAS QUE DEBES SABER / WORDS TO KNOW

(la) plataforma/
deck

(el) casco/
helmet

(las) coderas/elbow pads
(las) rodilleras/knee pads

ÍNDICE / INDEX

SITIOS DE INTERNET / WEBSITES

Due to the changing nature of Internet links, PowerKids Press has developed an online list of websites related to the subject of this book. This site is updated regularly. Please use this link to access the list: www.powerkidslinks.com/wmg/skbd